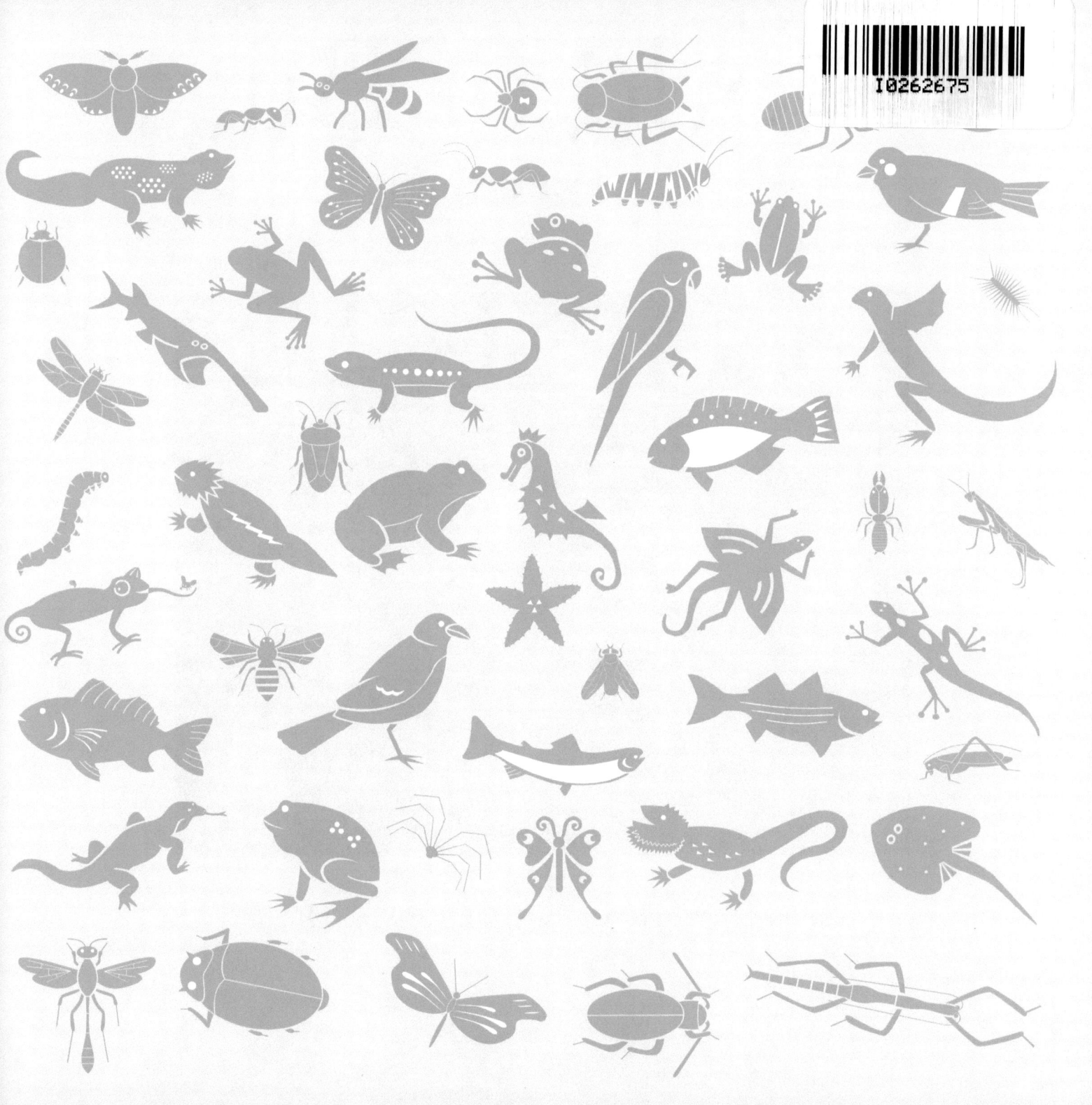

World of Bugs
Backyard Bugs

Concept and Design by Brandee Mae Hughes

All rights reserved.

This book or parts thereof may not be reproduced in any form, stored in a retrieval system, or transmitted in any form by any means – electronic, mechanical, photocopy, recording, or otherwise – without prior written permission of the author, except as provided by United States of America copyright law.

DISCLAIMER : All insects, bugs, arachnids and the like are referred to as "bugs" in this book for simplicity. Children should not handle insects without adult supervision as some bugs can cause severe injuries, even death, if not handled properly.

Text & Design ©2013 Brandee Mae Hughes Edited by: Crystal Murphy

Published in the United States of America

ISBN -10 # 0-9838295-6-x
ISBN -13 # 978-0-9838295-6-0

For information on other books and products, please visit our website at
http://www.BulaBug.com
or contact the author at **brandee@bulabug.com**

Follow Bula Bug on twitter @BulaBugs or by visiting www.twitter.com/BulaBugs
Like Bula Bug on Facebook at www.facebook.com/BulaBug

Bula Bug would love to include your photo in the next book. Enter the Photo Contest at www.bulabug.com to win. Winners will have their photos appear in one of the next *World of...* books.

Photo Contest Credits: Nanette Means – Contents page; Brandee Hughes – pg. 1, 3, 14, 62; Edward Zaydelman – pg. 4 (bottom right beetle); Patrick Jewell – pg. 9 (top left grasshopper); Judy Hooper – pg. 10 (top left caterpillar), 12 (bottom left milli-pede), 52 (top right caterpillars); Jesse Katz – pg. 39 (bottom right beetle); Cody Newman – pg. 40; Derek Rubinstein – pg. 66 (top left bee); Külli Kittus – pg. 67 (bottom left spider); Bruce Gregory – pg. 67 (top right bee); Laura Kim – pg. 85 (top left moths).

Contents:

What Bugs to look for 4
Bugs blend in 7
Where to look 12
Find Bugs on flowers 13
Find Bugs on plants and grass 26
Find Bugs on the ground 39
Find Bugs on bushes and trees 52
Possibly Dangerous Bugs 66

Always follow your dreams. Do what makes you happy. Find your smile and keep it shining. Stop and take time to notice the little things. Enjoy the beauty that is all around you. Treat others with love and respect. Be kind and understanding.

Insects live in many different places, and have many different faces. There are bugs with wings flying through the air. Bugs crawling around that are fuzzy and have hair. There are bugs that like to hide under rocks. Even bugs who like to eat socks. Bugs swimming in the lakes and rivers; bugs who creep and crawl and give you the shivers. There are bugs that glow in the dark, and bugs hiding in the grass at the park. Bugs who look like sticks and leaves, and bugs who look like bark on trees. In this book you will see where these tiny creatures might be!

What Bugs to Look for

Moth

Butterfly

Damselfly

Fly

Grasshopper

Snail

Dragonfly

Grub

Ladybug

Beetle

Woodlouse

Slug

Cricket

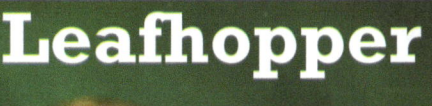
Leafhopper

Cicada

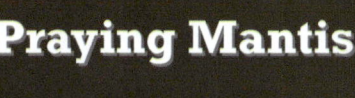
Praying Mantis

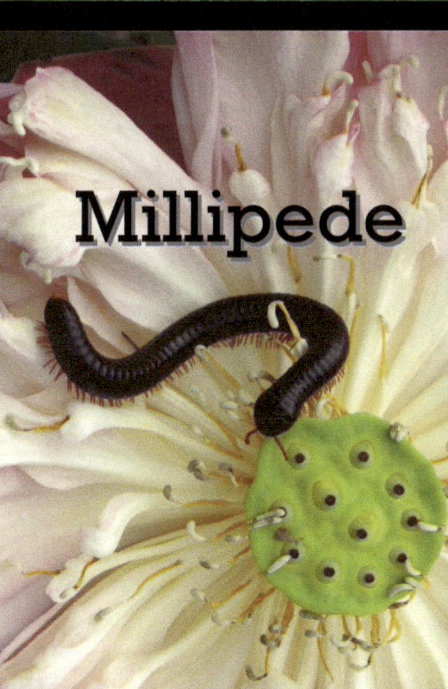
Millipede

Ant

Some bugs can be dangerous. They may bite or sting when they feel scared. Bugs are much smaller than us and can be scared easily. In this book you will see bugs that are safe to look for and bugs to stay away from. When looking for bugs, get a good look at them. Watch what they do and where they go. But do not touch them. Bugs do not like to be poked or squished. Bugs are tiny little creatures who live in our world with us. Show them respect and do not harm them. Bugs are our colorful little friends.

Bugs Blend In

Bugs survive by blending in with their environments. So look closely when you are searching for them...

These bugs look like leaves and flowers

These bugs look like wood and dirt.

These bugs look like branches and sticks.

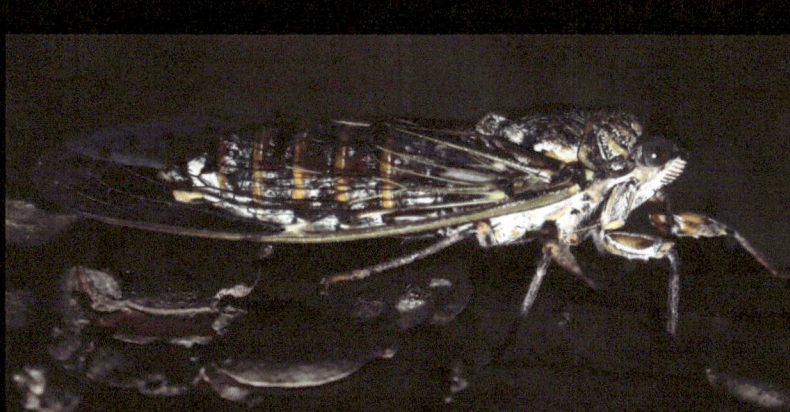

These bugs look like bark on trees.

Where to look

 Flowers

 Grass and Plants

 Rocky and Leafy Areas

 Bushes and Trees

Bugs like to hide in lots of different places outside. Flowers, rocky areas, grass, plants and trees are all great places to look. The little world of bugs is everywhere!

Find Bugs on Flowers

Praying Mantises

Grasshoppers

Butterflies

Beetles

Moths

Butterflies

The best place to find butterflies is near flowers. Butterflies can be found on all different types of blooms from roses to daisies. Butterflies drink the sweet nectar from the flowers with their long tongues.

Beetles

You can find beetles on and around flowers looking for food. Some of the things beetles eat include flower pollen, petals and leaves. Some beetles also eat smaller bugs that are found on flowers and plants.

Caterpillars

Caterpillars are often crawling around on plants near flowers eating leaves. Caterpillars crawl and crawl. Look for them on the stems or leaves of flowers. Caterpillars blend in with branches, leaves and stems. When searching for caterpillars, look carefully.

Find Bugs on Plants and Grass

Grasshoppers

Beetles

Damselflies

Praying Mantises

Caterpillars

Ladybugs

Grasshoppers

Grasshoppers are usually colored to match their environments. Some of the ones living in green grass are green. Other grasshoppers living in dry grass may be tan or brown. While some are bold and bright and don't blend in at all.

Damselflies

Damselflies love to soar through the sky. They fly from here to there but stop to rest now and then. They are most likely to be found flying around plants and trees near lakes, ponds and rivers.

Caterpillars

Caterpillars eat and eat. Their job is to eat as much as they can. Then as soon as they are big enough, they turn into butterflies and moths. You can find them on green plants and grass munching away.

Find Bugs on the Ground in Rocky and Leafy Areas

Millipedes

Grasshoppers

Praying Mantises

Snails

Beetles

Snails

Snails live on land and in fresh water. They also live deep in the sea. To find a snail on land, look near plants and gardens. Snails love to eat fresh green leaves at night and early in the morning.

Beetles

Beetles like to hide under rocks and leaves. They eat lots of things that can be found on the ground beneath the leaves, branches and rocks

Grasshoppers

Grasshoppers can be found resting on the ground blending in with the leaves and dirt around them. Watch closely, and you will see them hopping around the ground as you walk.

Find Bugs on Bushes and Trees

Lady Bugs

Moths

Caterpillars

Beetles

Dragonflies

Leafhoppers

Dragonflies

Dragonflies can be found flying around bushes and trees near rivers, lakes, ponds and streams. They also love wide-open spaces where they can soar through the sky. They fly very fast so watch closely.

Caterpillars

Caterpillars love to eat. They just keep eating! They snack on fresh new leaves from bushes and trees. Caterpillars like to hide, so be sure to look under the leaves.

Butterflies

Butterflies love to drink nectar from flowers. You can find them stopping for a drink on flowering trees and bushes. Butterflies also lay their eggs on the leaves of trees and bushes. That way their baby caterpillars have fresh leaves to eat when they hatch!

There are many bugs like the ones above that are safe to touch. There are also many that bite or sting, and some who even bite and sting! It is best to look at bugs, but not touch them. Touching certain bugs can be dangerous.

Possibly Dangerous Bugs

Bees

Spiders

Scorpions

It is best to keep your distance from certain bugs that may be dangerous. Here is a closer look at some of the bugs on the Possibly Dangerous list. These are bugs that may sting and/or bite, may have irritating hairs, or may be poisonous to touch

Spiders

There are many different varieties of spiders. Some spiders bite while others do not. Some spider bites can be deadly. It is best to look at spiders, but do not touch them.

Ants

Some ants may bite. Some may sting. Some ants even bite and sting, while other ants are harmless. It is best to watch how ants interact without touching them. Be careful when you see ants, because where there is one, there are usually many more.

Caterpillars

Some caterpillars have spikes or hairs that can be irritating to the skin or poisonous. Some spikes can even sting. So do not touch hairy or spikey caterpillars.

Wasps and Bees

Bees and wasps can all sting and bite. Be very careful if you see one. Slowly move away from them and never touch them.

 # Bug Hunt - Can You Find All 60 Bugs?

	7 Butterflies		3 Dragonflies		5 Caterpillars
	2 Praying Mantises		1 Damselfly		2 Centipedes
	3 Ladybugs		4 Bees/Wasps		4 Spiders
	9 Beetles		16 Ants		4 Grass Hoppers

When looking for bugs, make sure to look but not touch. Take time to watch what goes on, be patient and observe. There are amazing things to discover in the world of bugs.

We are always looking for new photos for our next book. If you like to take nature photos, enter them in the photo contest to win placement in one of our upcoming books.

Enter Today! www.bulabug.com/contest

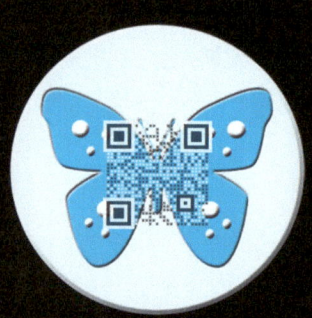

Nature Fun Store

Nature, Fun and Education www.BulaBug.com/store

There are special bug catchers that work great for catching bugs without touching them. To get a closer look, visit the Nature Fun Store at **BulaBug.com/store.**

You can also see butterflies, preying mantises and ladybugs grow up and watch ants build & maintain a home with special kits to raise insects.

Find bug viewers, bug houses and lots of bug catchers. There are puzzles, games, books and toys too!

The Bula Bug Nature Fun Store has everything you need to have fun while learning about nature.

Visit the Nature Fun Store today at BulaBug.com/store

The next book in the World of Bugs series is coming soon. **Stay updated!**

Follow Bula Bug's Blog bulabug.com

Like Bula Bug on Facebook

Follow Bula Bug on twitter

Collect all of the **World of** Books!

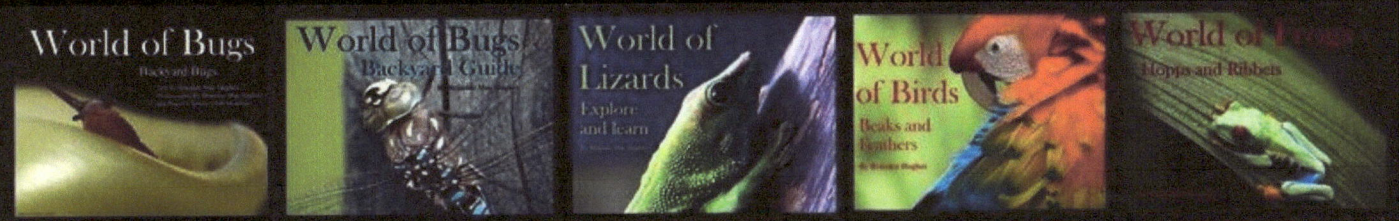

The "World of…" Series just keeps growing. There are more books coming soon! Visit BulaBug.com for more information about the books that are currently available.

 Would you like to suggest what type of creature we should feature in our next book?

 Do you have another question or suggestion? Send us your suggestions!

 Do you have something else you would like to tell us or discuss?

We would love to know your thoughts!

Email us: thoughts@bulabug.com
Call us: 916.760.7699
Send us a Letter: P.O. Box 90 Auburn, CA 95603
Send us a Fax: 916.760.8458
Facebook Message us: www.facebook.com/BulaBug
Message us on Twitter: www.twitter.com/BulaBugs

www.ingramcontent.com/pod-product-compliance
Lightning Source LLC
Chambersburg PA
CBHW042035150426
43201CB00002B/28